ODYSSEY OF A JEWISH SAILOR

Captain F Ashe Lincoln
Q.C. RNVR

MINERVA PRESS
MONTREUX LONDON WASHINGTON

ODYSSEY OF A JEWISH SAILOR
Copyright © F Ashe Lincoln 1995

All Rights Reserved

ISBN 1 85863 600 0

First Published 1995 by
MINERVA PRESS
10 Cromwell Place
London SW7 2JN

Printed in Great Britain by
B.W.D. Ltd., Northolt, Middlesex

ODYSSEY OF A JEWISH SAILOR

I dedicate this book to my beloved wife, the true heroine who had to wait and worry.

THE NAVAL CAREER OF CAPTAIN ASHE LINCOLN

1935   Joined Naval Reserve

1939   Commissioned as Sub-Lt RNVR for active service
        with the Royal Navy

1939   September to October HMS Vernon for mine training

1939   Mid October to mid November, served at sea in
        Minelayers

1939   Mid November summoned to Admiralty to investigate
        magnetic mines

1940   January, appointed no. One, Mine Investigating
        Section, Admiralty

1942   Promoted Lt-Commander
        King's Commendation for bravery for rendering safe
        new type magnetic mines

1943   Mediterranean Campaign with 30 Commando
        mentioned in Despatches for assault on Salerno

1944   February to June, USA and Pacific. Work on
        invasion beaches in Seine Bay.

1945   First Naval Officer across the Rhine

1945   March, Promoted to Commander

1945-
1946   North Germany, minesweeping in the Baltic

1947   Became King's Counsel

1948   Formed Israeli Navy

FOREWORD
By Chief Rabbi Sacks

Ashe Lincoln Q.C. is one of the most delightful people it
has been my privilege to get to know. An outstanding barrister
and a prominent member of the Anglo-Jewish community, he is
a man of charm and good humour who has devoted much of a
long lifetime to the service of others. But the quality I most
admire in him is that he is a man of faith, one who has always
been proud of his Jewish religious heritage and who has lived
out that faith in difficult circumstances in an exemplary way.
That is what makes this volume of wartime memoirs such
inspiring reading.

War brings out the worst in the bad and the best in the good.
It is impossible to read ODYSSEY OF A JEWISH SAILOR
without realising that Ashe Lincoln is a very good man indeed.
He is modest about his achievements and generous in his praise
of others. But these reminiscences of the Second World War
and of Israel's struggle for independence are remarkable for
their quiet courage and for the story they tell about how one
man found strength in his faith, and through it was able to give
strength and help to others. This is a book to cherish.

The Psalmist speaks of those who "go down to the sea in
ships, ply their trade in the mighty waters; they have seen the
works of the Lord and His wonders in the deep" (Psalm 107:
23-24). Those words could serve as Ashe's message to his
readers. This is the work of a man who served the British navy
with distinction, and the Jewish people with deep dedication. I
feel honoured to count him as a friend.

Dr Jonathan Sacks
Chief Rabbi of the United Hebrew Congregations of the
Commonwealth
Purim Katan 5755
14th February 1995

PREFACE

There is a unique spiritual link implicit in the sea. Is not the very first mention of the Divine Spirit in the awful moment of Creation that it "moved on the face of waters"? How vividly can one experience this from the Ship's Bridge when on the morning watch, just before dawn, the vast restless ocean stretches out to the very rim of the world and in the silent moment before sunrise, a little breeze comes whispering over the empty waters.

There is comfort in that little breeze, for though in that vast expanse the ship may seem lonely yet Death may lurk unseen beneath the waters. These things I have known and am glad to write some of the incidents of many turbulent years.

Looking back, I am indeed happy that I was born a Jew to inherit the traditions of the House of Israel and to contribute in my own small way to its history.

Proud and happy am I also that it was my good fortune to be born British, to be part of this great Imperial people imbued with a firm Christian ethic which is after all identical to our Jewish ideal from which it is derived and which has spread civilised Law and Order over most of the globe.

PART 1

CHAPTER 1

September 3rd 1939 was a bright sunny morning. I had taken my two children to the farm of the James family on the hill behind our house in Somerset. The children were still babes - my daughter was just 4 and my son would be 2 in a few days. Even as they excitedly watched the cows being herded out to graze, I knew that long separation faced us, for over the weekend the news of Hitler's wanton attack on Poland had startled the world. When therefore the farmer ran out to tell us that Neville Chamberlain was to broadcast to the nation at 11 o'clock, it could mean only one thing - WAR! I was already in the Royal Naval Volunteer Supplementary Reserve and this meant an immediate call-up.

On our way back to the house I reflected that the Jewish New Year (Rosh Hashana) would be in five days. How like Hitler, I thought, to start a war in such a week. So here was my first problem. Anxious as I was to get into active service in this war against evil, I felt nevertheless that hostilities would last well over a week and I might fairly ask the Navy for a week at home before being formally enrolled.

The next day I drove my father back to London. The air-raid warnings of the previous day had not materialised into the devastating attack we all anticipated after Warsaw had been so cruelly laid waste. At home the call-up notice was on the mat to report forthwith. I telephoned the Admiralty to request a week's grace which was kindly given. I need not have worried because established Admiralty Orders provided for automatic leave for all Jewish personnel for the New Year and for the Day of Atonement, so I would have had leave anyway.

The day after the New Year I was duly commissioned in H.M.S. King Alfred as a sub-lieutenant RNVR. There was one other Jew in our enrolment, the Hon Ewen Montagu, whom I had known as a colleague at the Bar and who was destined to go on to a distinguished career in the Service, though at that time none of us had any inkling of what awaited us in the years ahead.

Two weeks later I was in H.M.S. Vernon, the mining and torpedo school at Portsmouth, training to be a specialist in mines and underwater weapons. I was of course still a humble sub-lieutenant. I thought I ought to notify the Jewish chaplaincy that I was serving in the Royal Navy. That area of communal activity was under the direction of Dayan Gollop whom I had known well in London, where I had taken a leading part in such movements as the Sabbath Observance group for young people as well as an active role in Zionist work. I had toured the country with Locker-Lampson MP in a campaign to boycott German goods because of Hitler's anti-Semitism. I was therefore somewhat surprised to receive from the learned Dayan a small book of Jewish Thoughts with a abbreviated Siddur (Prayer Book) and a letter which said, "I do not know whether you know anything about religious observance etc." I was also appalled because the letter was addressed to Captain Lincoln, a rank in the Royal Navy of considerable eminence. Indeed in H.M.S. Vernon there was only the one Captain in Command before whom I was promptly hailed to explain how I had dared to represent myself as a Captain. I explained the position to Captain Boyd who was very amused and was kind enough to accept my defence. The whole incident, however, left me far from well disposed towards the chaplaincy department, with whom I carefully avoided further contact during the rest of my service.

However, this event was to have strong influence on my career in the Service. When some 2 months later Captain Dennis Boyd was summoned to the Admiralty by Churchill who was then First Lord of the Admiralty and directed to work as Chief of Staff to Admiral Wake-Walker to discover an answer to the German magnetic mine, both these officers decided they needed, "someone with a legal mind who knew something about mines". Captain Boyd remembered me from H.M.S.

Vernon and had me recalled from sea to join his new
investigation team. I have no doubt that this was the result of
the Dayan's gaffe.

CHAPTER 2

No account of my experiences would be complete without mention of some of the remarkable men who were fellow Jews with whom I had special contact in the Navy. I have already mentioned the Hon Ewen Montagu whose distinguished service especially in his special intelligence work is well known.

I, however, mean to relate the exploits of those Jews who were immediately under my command or were working in close association with me.

In 1940 we had established at the Admiralty in London the section known as DTM I. This was the investigation section of the Department of Torpedoes and Mines and was concerned with these particular enemy weapons. We had to locate enemy minefields at sea and discover what type of mine was in them. Also we had to render safe any unexploded mine ashore either on the beaches or if dropped from enemy aircraft at any place. Many of the earlier magnetic mines were in fact dropped inland or were used as bombs in the various blitzes on our cities. Where these monsters were lying unexploded, it was our task to find them and in conjunction with Vernon parties operating from Portsmouth to render them safe. Vernon covered the South Coast; we were responsible for the rest of the country. I was number one of this section. On our staff we had some mine experts and some who specialised in Torpedoes.

As number one I had to qualify in both weapons to advise on and in general deal with any new specimen. When we were building up the section we had to find volunteers who were willing to take on these unusual and especially hazardous tasks. Not everyone can face a live mine which might explode at any moment and retain sufficiently calm emotion to remove the fuses and other sensitive parts slowly and deliberately. But this was essential.

One day the Admiralty was approached by one Saunders, a Jew, who had served in the war of 1914-1918 in MTB's and had won the DSO and was de-mobbed with the rank of Lt-Cmdr. Now in 1940 he wanted desperately to get back into the Navy, but he was in his late forties and was considered too old for service. However, he persisted and was then asked if he would volunteer to render mines safe. He gladly agreed and was given the rank of Lieut. RNVR and joined our party. He had of course to be sent for initial training but that being completed he joined us in time to take part in the mammoth tasks that followed the blitz on London and elsewhere. He became so efficient that we were able to entrust him with important jobs and this in the end led to his narrow escape from death. It came about in this way.

After a night of a heavy bombing attack on London, I left my digs by Regents Park to find immediately outside the block that there was a crater strewn with the parts of a magnetic mine. I immediately contacted the police and air raid wardens nearby to enquire the whereabouts of its companion as these parachute mines were always dropped in pairs. The other was lying unexploded in Camden Town. I telephoned to Capt. Maitland-Dougall, our chief at the Admiralty, to ask for my set of non-magnetic tools to be sent up to me at once. But the Captain was most clearly in desperate need of me at the Admiralty as he told me there were no less than 150 mines lying around London and the suburbs and parties had to be urgently organised.

At HQ we were faced with the problem that we could only muster in London a total of 5 trained officers and we needed 2 for each mine. An urgent call had already been sent to H.M.S. Vernon, the mine school at Portsmouth, who said they had despatched 30 trained petty officers to help us. Every call was urgent and we had assigned Lt-Cmdr R Ryan RN to go at once to Dagenham. Saunders was assigned to help him. As they turned to go through the door the Vernon petty officers arrived. We therefore told Ryan to choose one of them to be his assistant and release Saunders for another job. Such is the working of Providence, for both Ryan and his petty officer were unhappily blown to pieces and the news of their death left us shocked and in the deepest mourning as we grimly set about clearing the rest of the mines. Saunders successfully dealt with his mines and survived the War.

Another officer who was working on this rendering safe task was Lt Newgass RNVR. He was in many ways a rather strange character. He was a Jew but almost completely assimilated. His home was in some remote part of the West country where he aped the country gentleman. He always wore a monocle which went well with his aloof semi-aristocratic mannerisms. Nevertheless he was of outstanding courage and ability and carried out an exploit which must always rank as one of the most brave in the whole war.

The story of it was that after the great blitz on the Mersey area, one mine had fallen on a gasometer and was swinging in the gas from its parachute which was caught on the roof. This gasometer was adjacent to a munitions factory so that an explosion would have had more than usual devastating consequences. Newgass had himself fitted into a diving suit so that he could be lowered in to swing beside the mine and remove the fuse and primer. Bearing in mind that if the clockwork fuse began to run, there was not the slightest chance of escape, he knew perfectly well the full extent of the hazard he faced. We must ever salute this achievement and I have always felt proud to have known him. For this exploit he was awarded the George Cross. He was afterwards promoted Lt-Cmdr. He continued his rendering safe work and happily survived the War.

CHAPTER 3

In 1942 the Germans carried out a great blitz on Plymouth which was my home town. Night after night for ten days the three towns of Plymouth, Stonehouse and Devonport were mercilessly and incessantly bombed to the extent that they were virtually obliterated. Street after street of houses, shops and offices were reduced to rubble and casualties were high.

As was usual with such blitz attacks, the enemy used large numbers of parachute mines because of their additional destructive power. I was therefore sent with a small party to cope with the problems of rendering safe any unexploded mines, of which there were several. My particular duty also involved advising Captain Hodson, Captain of Minesweepers, on the necessary measures to keep the channels seaward of Devonport Naval Dockyard clear of mines and available to vital traffic. In consequence my Headquarters were with the Minesweepers in Millbay Docks.

Working ashore to deal with the unexploded mines, I was able to see the pitiful sight of the population streaming out of the town at night to take refuge in the safer areas of Dartmoor.

There were two mines in particular which I had to deal with personally, one of which had fallen and lay unexploded just inside the gates of Devonport Park. By coincidence, this was at the end of a street known as Stoke Villas where my grandparents had lived. Working on this mine, therefore, had particular nostalgic appeal to me. Another mine lay unexploded just outside the front door of the Admiral's house at Mount Wise, and after I had dealt with that, the Admiral invited me to join him and his family for lunch.

The Admiral was Admiral Dunbar-Naismith VC. It was fascinating to hear his first hand account of how, as a Submarine Commander, he had won his Victoria Cross in the 1914-18 War. He had boldly and courageously taken his

Submarine through Turkish minefields to penetrate the heart of the scene of operations in the Gallipoli Campaign.

Here, I must digress to mention the fact that having been invited to lunch, I requested that I might have fish, which was readily forthcoming. During the whole of my Service in the Royal Navy, I endeavoured as far as possible to observe our religious laws in relation to diet. Obviously, this was not always possible, but it was worth the effort even though on one occasion at sea, in a Destroyer, I had to exist on mashed potatoes for most meals.

One amusing sideline was that when I was serving with the Marine Commando in the Sicilian and Italian Campaign, we were issued with the standard American field rations which were known as K rations. These ration packs had in them tins of ham as well as tins of sardines. I was able to achieve popularity with the Marines by swapping my ham for their sardines.

Immediately after lunch, I had to return hurriedly to the Docks and instructed my Wren driver to drive me first to the Naval Dockyard at Devonport in order to ascertain the position there. On leaving the Dockyard gates, I remembered that in one of the adjoining streets, Chapel Street, there had been a small temporary synagogue which my grandfather had established when he became too old and ill to walk to the Plymouth Synagogue. There had of course, been a synagogue in Devonport as far back as the days of the Napoleonic Wars. At that time, Devonport was known by the name of "Plymouth Dock" and the old spice box bearing the Plymouth Dock inscription is still in possession of the Plymouth Hebrew Congregation. However, by the middle of the 19th Century, the old Synagogue in Devonport had disappeared and the new temporary one was created by my grandfather much later about 1909.

All this was flashing through my mind as we left the Dockyard gates. I knew that if we could drive through Chapel Street, we would be on our route back to Millbay Docks. It occurred to me suddenly, that I might look at the ruins of the building in which the Synagogue had stood if we could find it. The first problem was to find Chapel Street itself, which was not easy in the mass of rubble. However, after a short while, my Wren driver found what we took to be Chapel Street and we drove along it slowly. When we came to the spot at which I thought the Synagogue had been, I saw a gang of workmen who were clearing the debris. Accordingly, I stopped the car and went across to ask them whether they had discovered anything which by chance had belonged to the Synagogue. One of them took me to an area they had partially cleared and there, sticking out of the rubble, I could see the top of the two wooden supports of a Sefer Torah. I asked the men to dig carefully round it, which they obligingly did and we were able to unearth the whole Scroll which seemed undamaged but without a cover of any kind. I took the remains of a German mine parachute which we tore apart to make a temporary wrapping and accordingly laid the Sefer in the back seat of the car. There appeared to be nothing else that we could find.

On the way back to the Docks to rejoin the Minesweepers, we drove past the Police Station. I took the Sefer Torah into the Station and gave it into the care of the Superintendent there, asking him to convey it as soon as he could, to the Rabbi, Rev Goodman in Plymouth. This he readily agreed to do. I accordingly returned to join the minesweepers, feeling at least, that I had done my Mitzvah for the day.

One incident in connection with the rendering safe of mines is especially worth recording.

One of my officers rendered safe a German magnetic mine which appeared to be of a usual type. When, however, the mine was opened and examined, it was found that it would never have operated as a mine because the whole of the internal works had been sabotaged. Furthermore, on the inside of the mine casing, the explanation appeared. Someone had drawn a shield of David (Magen David) and underneath in English had put the words, "We are with you". Clearly this was the work of a Jewish forced labourer who was being used as one of the slave labourers by the Nazis in their munitions factory. The risk that he or she had taken was enormous because quite clearly, to deliberately sabotage a weapon in that way under the very noses of the Nazis, involved a risk of execution. Nevertheless, it was a very heartening thing for us to realise that even at the risk of their own lives, these unhappy slaves were willing to save the lives of our fighters and ships. We reported this finding directly to the Prime Minister, Winston Churchill, who wisely ordered that the most scrupulous secrecy must be observed about the incident, because as he put it, if it became public knowledge, there would undoubtedly ensue a wholesale massacre of slave labourers. Of course, we did not wish to throw away the undoubted advantage that this type of sabotage gave to us. There is a strong probability that sabotage of this kind was frequently practised by slave labourers as far as they could in many different types of weapon. However, this particular example stood out because so far as I am aware, it was the only case in which a message had been inscribed making clear the originator of the sabotage.

CHAPTER 4
OPERATION TEFILLIN

I have always found that observance of the Mitzvah of laying Tefillin, has throughout my life given me great pleasure. It is an observance of a unique character which gives tone and meaning to the day ahead. I was therefore resolved from the very moment of receiving my call-up notice for the Royal Navy that I should maintain this practice. Fortunately, I was able to do so, except for one or two occasions during the whole of my active Service.

When I was with other Reserve Officers enrolled in HMS King Alfred, we were billeted in accommodation which had virtually no privacy. I fully appreciated that commencing the day with traditional prayers and Tefillin would look strange to my fellow Officers and might involve a certain amount of ridicule. However, I found that when I explained to them the significance of what I was doing and reminded them of the direct biblical injunction "to wear them (these words) as a sign upon your hand and as a frontlet between your eyes", they were interested and respectful. One or two instances in this connection stand out particularly.

In November, 1942, I found myself ordered to investigate a new German minefield in the North Sea. At that time I had the rank of Lieutenant Commander and was number 1 of the Navy section investigating enemy mines and underwater weapons. This new minefield had given indications of a variation in the sensitivity of the German magnetic mine and it was my duty to observe at first hand, the effects of our standard method of sweeping this type of mine. Accordingly, I had command of a flotilla of mine sweepers which I had to lead into the minefield in question. I was in the principal ship of the flotilla which was HMS Rolls Royce, which had already established a reputation as the champion mine sweeper of the Home Fleet. Evidence that we were facing a new type of mine was not long in coming, because although with our standard sweep, each ship had a wide area of protective magnetic field about it, we had the horror of seeing our accompanying sweeper blown up with the loss of all its crew. Very shortly afterwards, a mine exploded barely 150 feet astern of our own ship. We had nevertheless to continue the investigation and sweeping in order to have a clear channel safe for the next southbound convoy. I had therefore, to remain on the bridge until nearly mid-night by which time, it was possible for me to turn in. However, just as I was about to do so, we were heavily attacked by a flotilla of German motor torpedo boats and in consequence, I was unable to get to my bunk until 2.00am. When I finally turned in, the wind was increasing and all the indications were that we were in for a November gale. Each ship was only a small converted trawler of about 150 to 200 tons and the consequent motion in the ensuing gale was particularly violent. When I awoke about 6.30am I decided that I would lay Tefillin, but the gale was at its height and it was virtually impossible to stand upright in the cabin and in fact, I had to say my prayers by resting my feet on the cabin wall and my head on the bunk. I am sure I shall be forgiven for the fact that my Dovening was somewhat curtailed.

Another occasion worth recalling was when in 1943 I was serving in the Mediterranean with number 30 Marine Commando. This was an unusual and special Commando which was entirely under the jurisdiction of the Royal Navy and not part of the Combined Forces. The Commando consisted of some 500 Marines and an Army section of 200 to 350 men; the whole Commando being under the command of Naval Officers. It was designated a special Assault Unit for the purpose of the Royal Navy. We had taken part in the invasion of Sicily from North Africa and fought throughout the Sicilian campaign. By the beginning of September 1943, we were assigned to be one of the Commandoes to carry out the assault on Salerno on the Italian mainland. The particular task to which I had been designated was to carry out the assault on the Port of Salerno and to render safe the demolition charges on the port installations so that the Port would remain usable. However, as our convoy proceeded across, we were attacked by Italian torpedo carrying aircraft who succeeded in damaging one of the LCT's so that the troops had to be redistributed between the various ships. As a result of this, the American overall command split our Commando into two. Oddly enough, this successful attack by Italian aircraft only came a day or two before the Italian surrender. As a result of the re-arrangement of the troops, when we ultimately arrived in the Bay of Salerno, I found that my particular section had to make an assault landing many miles down the coast from Salerno itself, in fact, at the old Roman town of Paestum. We had anticipated that there would be little opposition in view of the Italian surrender but we had not allowed for the rapidity in which the German forces were able to redeploy. Our assault landings were to take place after dark at 2.00am and in accordance with standard practice, I stood with the Colour Sergeant at the head of the Marines in the darkened landing craft at the base of the drawbridge at the bow. The drill was that the moment the landing craft grounded and the drawbridge dropped, we were to charge out across the beach. As we moved on towards the beach, the Colour Sergeant turned to me and said, "Is it not strange, Sir, that you a Jew and me a Christian are likely to die together in the next few minutes?" However, we successfully landed and charged up the beach through the hail of machine gun fire. There is probably nothing more unnerving than to see the streams of tracer bullets which greet you on such an occasion. We managed to reach some shelter behind the sand dunes and the grassy slopes behind which, even in the night light we could see the columns of the ruined Roman town. We bivouacked down, quite exhausted for the night in the open field. When I awoke the next morning, I was struck by a very remarkable incident because, clear as a clarion call, across the fields, came the sound of a cockerel hailing the new day and hearing this above the screech of the shells that were coming from the German artillery, my instant reaction was to murmur the traditional blessing from the commencement of our daily prayers, "Blessed art Thou O Lord our God who has given to the cockerel understanding to distinguish between day and night". The German artillery had somehow found more or less, the exact range of our field and at regular intervals, a shell was lobbed into our midst. It was essential therefore that everyone should lie low to avoid the ensuing shrapnel. I got my Tefillin out of my haversack and took shelter under the rear of one of our armoured cars which we had successfully landed the night before and which provided me at least with some shelter whilst standing to say the Amedah. My Marines round about me expressed that they were considerably cheered by my praying and said that somehow or other it had made them feel more secure. My devotions over, the Colour Sergeant crept up to me to say that he had scouted out the position roundabout and had sighted the German observations post which was clearly directing their artillery fire onto our position. He and I then took a couple of Bren guns out to the perimeter and were able to dispose of the German observation post with a few well directed bursts from the Brens, which on this fortunate occasion did not jamb at the vital moment of firing.

I have mentioned that I maintained my customary Tefillin as regularly as possible, but there were two definite occasions on which I had to forgo the pleasure. One of these occasions was during the Commando operations in Sicily, when I had the misfortune to sustain a slight wound through my left hand on the occasion that we raided the Italian base at Trapani. We had no Doctor on this raid and the best that could be done for me was a hasty bandage from one of the Marines and a home made sling. It was, in fact, some days before I was able to get the proper medical attention and my left arm and hand had to be in a sling for three weeks.

Another occasion occurred on the night of Montgomery's assault across the Rhine in 1944. At the time, I was charged with the duty of ensuring the protection of the assault boats on the river from German mines that were being floated down the Rhine. On the night of the assault, therefore, I had to carry out the last minute investigations along our own banks to ensure the safety of the assault boats. On this tour, along the front, I was accompanied by a Colonel of General Simpson's Ninth Army, which was the American Army on the right flank of the assault. The American Colonel provided a jeep and driver who conducted us along the miles of section at the juncture of the American and British troops. I had confidently believed that I could carry out the instructions of the many duties with sufficient time to get back to my Headquarters billet, but as events unfolded, it became clear that I would have to continue my vigil and conduct the operation on the banks of the River itself until after the very moment of the assault itself, which took place in the early hours of the morning. Movements were considerably hampered by the heavy mortar shelling from the Germans, whom we could see on the opposite bank. At one moment they succeeded in landing a mortar shell so near to our jeep that our driver received a slight wound to his shoulder. The result of spending the whole night in the course of these operations meant that by the following morning, I had to continue on the other side of the River and was unable, in fact, to get back to my own billet for a further 24 hours to collect my Tefillin.

Whilst patrolling the Riverbank, I entered a pillbox which was being used as a forward observations post by the Army. Upon entering, I was greeted by a young Jewish Army Lieutenant, who introduced himself as Lt Amswych, whose family I knew well in London. Indeed, it was his father's firm which had supplied the carpets for the matrimonial home of my wife and myself on our wedding.

CHAPTER 5

The year 1943 began unhappily. I had become ill and though I struggled to keep going, it soon became apparent to my Captain that I was not able to continue my responsible duties but was in urgent need of medical treatment. It was a combination of war weariness with the resultant heavy strain of the hazards involved in dealing with unexploded weapons of new types and the deep emotional stress of losing friends who became victims in the struggle. Both the Captain and I could not but feel a sense of responsibility when we had ordered an officer to carry out an investigation of a weapon and he lost his life while doing his duty. Of course it was not our fault, but the loss was always keenly felt as a personal hurt. All this the Doctors said caused me to develop severe gall bladder trouble and I was sent first to the Royal Naval hospital at Chatham. There the Matron informed me that my treatment would involve a special diet and, "we have no time for that sort of thing". Accordingly I was removed to the Royal Masonic hospital at Ravenscourt Park in London which had been partially given over to the Forces. There a surgeon Rear Admiral Wakely decided rapidly that surgery, to remove my gall bladder, was essential. This was accordingly done. In those days medical treatment was not as advanced as it later became and my convalescence was slow. In the result the Rear-Admiral decreed that I was to be off active service for 6 months!!

That was fine; I could have Pesach at home. But the War was still on and in the Mediterranean, preparations were being made for the invasion of Sicily. Obviously Marine commandos were going to be involved. There was one special commando number 30 which belonged to the Royal Navy and did not come under the command of Combined Forces which controlled the other Royal Marine commandos. Number 30 was reserved for any special task which the Navy required. It was thought that here was a unique opportunity to use this commando to go after enemy weapons depots. If therefore I would go with it, I could pursue my investigations of enemy weapons by actually seizing them. This obviously was better than waiting in an Admiralty office for intelligence to filter through. Thus within 6 weeks of my operation, I found myself assigned to 30 Commando and was kitted out for the forthcoming Mediterranean campaign. I was still too weak to undergo the full commando training and had to make do with training in small arms revolver, rifle and Bren guns etc.

I was given Lt Ogle as my staff officer and then had to wait the actual time of departure which I was permitted to do on leave. I therefore asked my wife to come to London to spend a day or two with me prior to what I knew would be a long separation. I did not tell her that I was joining the commandos and obviously could not say anything of the intended operations in the Med. There was no point, I felt, in worrying her unduly and what was in the wind was highly secret. The most I could say was that I was going abroad. However, one evening we were in a cinema together, when suddenly the movie was interrupted by a flash on the screen: "Lt-Cmdr Ashe Lincoln is to report to the Admiralty at once". I had of course informed the Admiralty that I was going to a cinema and this order was flashed to all cinemas to catch me. Telephoning to the Admiralty I was told I would be duly collected by a staff car to be taken to a plane. For my wife therefore, the secret of my commando appointment was soon out because on return to my digs I had to get into my commando rig and pack my tropical gear. She was used to shocks like that, because when I had been first appointed to the Admiralty she had naturally assumed that I was getting a cushy shore job and it was only when the press published that I had received the Kings commendation for bravery that she got an inkling of the kind of job I was doing. Now I had to say a hasty good-bye and I was off.

We were first flown to Cornwall where we were to join a number of others to be flown to Gibraltar. We sat around in a rather sombre circle in the gloom of a blacked-out hut on the edge of the airfield. One by one our names were called and we had to name next-of-kin and their address and our religion. One after the other it was "C of E" and then me the sole Jew.

From Gibraltar we were flown to Algiers, but HQ there had no idea where we should find 30 Commando. Ultimately we found them under canvas. The commanding officer was Lt-Cmdr Quintin Riley. We introduced ourselves to him in the evening of our arrival and showed him the Admiralty orders governing the circumstances under which I was to have the commando at my disposal. It was clear that Riley was not at all pleased and I took care to assure him that we should do everything together in a spirit of amity for the great cause we both had at heart. But worse was to come. Riley was a remarkable character. He held both the Arctic and the Antarctic medals, having been the hero of some notable expeditions in one of which he was the only officer to survive. He was autocratic in manner and in his attitude to his men. He was fiercely religious as an Anglo-Catholic and told Ogle and me that he insisted that everyone should kneel during morning prayers. I told him that while I respected his religion, I expected equal respect for mine and that as a Jew I would certainly not kneel. His response was a sudden outburst, "My God I hate all Jews."

I replied, "That is a pity; you will have to tolerate this one as we have to go through a campaign together." It is satisfying to record that by the end of the campaign, we were firm friends and remained so to the end of his life. When years after the War Quintin's father died and there was a memorial service for him in St Margarets church, Westminster, Quintin asked me to join his family in the special pew reserved for them.

CHAPTER 6

TO THE RESCUE

In 1943 my 30 Marine Commando had established its base on the shores of the Adriatic just outside the port of Bari. From there, we were regularly taking arms to the underground fighters in Yugoslavia. By the end of October, our orders were to supply these arms to the forces of Tito diverting them from the forces of General Mihailovic. This was as a result of a political decision at the highest level. Our contacts with the forces of Tito were in the Island of Vis where we had established a base. On one of these forays, I was informed by Tito's Officers that in the islands in the north of the Adriatic, there were some 4,000 refugees from Croatia. The information we had about Croatia itself at that time indicated that the Ustashe, which was a fascist movement in Croatia, was co-operating fully with the Germans and was virulently anti-Jewish. Indeed, so brutal and cruel were the Croatians towards the Jews that it was reported that even the German SS protested. When, therefore, I heard that there were 4,000 refugees from Croatia hiding in the islands, it was almost certain that they would be Jewish refugees.

The other alarming intelligence was to the effect that German forces were actively moving to expel Tito's partisans from these islands and I was asked whether it would be possible to send strong detachments from my Commando to strengthen the defences of the islands. It was apparent to me that I could not at that time muster anything like a force strong enough in number or equipment to withstand determined German attacks on those islands. I did, however, send a small detachment under the command of Lt-Cmdr Guy Morgan in order to see what could be done to organise an effective defence, but this in the end proved futile and Morgan himself was wounded and captured by the Germans. However, it seemed to me that if, as appeared probable, the islands were going to be retaken by the Germans, the most immediate steps were required to ensure the safety of the refugees. I accordingly approached Commander Wellman of the Royal Navy who was in command of the Coastal forces in the Southern Adriatic and explained the problem to him. I had hardly got through my opening remarks about the peril of the refugees and the violence of the Ustashe when Wellman cut me short by saying, "I fully appreciate the perilous position of the Jews because my wife is Jewish". He therefore was very willing to give me every possible assistance within his power. He provided a flotilla of 6 motor gun boats, one of which by chance was commanded by a Jewish Officer, Lt-Cmdr Romain, whose family I had known in London. I was able by radio to instruct my Detachment in the islands to put the refugees into such boats as they could commandeer and dispatch them as quickly as possible to Southern Italy. I was assured that these boats, fully manned and crowded as they were, would rendezvous with the gunboats who would escort them safely to Bari.

In the meanwhile, some arrangement had to be made ashore with the British authorities for the reception of such a large party. There were contingents of the Guards in Bari and I approached their Colonel explaining the problem and he immediately offered the fullest co-operation on humanitarian grounds. He arranged for his Guards to take over some empty Italian barracks and also organised medical staff because we had to assume that the health of these refugees might well have been imperilled by their unhappy experiences. Our precautions turned out to be fully justified because when the party arrived, many of the younger women were pregnant and it is to the everlasting credit of the Army authorities that everything possible was done to ensure the welfare of the refugees.

Once their immediate safety was assured, it was clear that they could not be left as a burden upon the military authorities who were of course, still fully engaged with the necessary operations to clear the rest of Italy of the German armies. I was able to get into touch with Alec Easterman of the World Jewish Congress in London and inform him of the position. He, with his usual energy, immediately enlisted the assistance of the American Joint Distribution Committee, who had the funds to organise and care for a refugee problem of this kind.

The longer term had still, of course, to be considered and urgent representations were made by the World Jewish Congress and the Zionist Federation in London to the Prime Minister and as a result of their efforts, special permits were issued to enable the whole body to enter Palestine.

It was an interesting sequel to these events that when in 1948 I was in Palestine prior to the establishment of the State of Israel, organising a Naval force which was to be the nucleus of the Israeli Navy, I was one day accosted by a young member of the Haganah who said that he had been a boy among these refugees in Italy and remembered me from those days.

Another occasion of rescue was to occur still later in the following year, 1944. I had taken part in the invasion of France in the Seine Bay operations in June of 1944 and as the invasion proceeded, I found myself inevitably moved up the coast until we were able to enter Belgium itself. At the time of the taking of Brussels, I had had to take over the work of the clearance of the airfield at Melsbrook where accompanied by Lt Broome, we had jointly rendered safe some 150 German mines which were stored at the Airport awaiting German Aircraft Minelayers. I had to return to London to report on these operations and whilst at the Admiralty was contacted by Rabbi Schonfeld, who told me the following tale.

A member of his community in London had a sister and brother-in-law who had been in hiding in Brussels at the time of the German invasion. For a while this couple, who had a child, had been in hiding with their son, shielded by friendly Belgians. However, unfortunately, after a while, their whereabouts had been discovered by the Gestapo and when the couple realised that they would be removed to a concentration camp, they had put their little boy into the care of some nuns who undertook to look after him and protect him. So far as the family in London were concerned, their information was that the young couple had met their inevitable fate in the death camps of the Nazis, but they were anxious to trace the child and I was asked if I could make enquiries through the Belgian Police to discover his whereabouts and if possible, get him restored to the family in London. Naturally, I agreed to do what I could and upon my return to Belgium in a few days, I put the case to the Chief of Police in Brussels who undertook to investigate and report to me as soon as he could. Shortly afterwards, he reported that he had found the boy, but the nuns stated that he had been baptised and converted to Roman Catholicism and that they refused to give him up. The Belgian Police were very sympathetic to the claims of the family in the circumstances and brought the necessary pressure to bear. Ultimately they were able to inform me that the boy was available and with the help of the British authorities, he was put on a boat for transfer to Dover. I was able to convey this happy information to Rabbi Schonfeld who arranged to collect the boy at Dover, which was in due course successfully accomplished.

Much later I learnt of the outcome. It appeared that the boy was taken to the home of his grandparents. At the evening meal when the grandfather said grace, the boy made the sign of the cross which caused considerable consternation, but was only to be expected, with regard to his upbringing to that date.

Years later, after the War was all over, I happened to be a guest of the late Rabbi Kopul Rosen at the school which he had founded - namely Carmel College. The occasion was the annual prize giving and certain chosen scholars came to the platform to recite in Hebrew a Psalm. One boy in particular was outstanding and as he left the platform, a lady emerged from the crowd of families and parents and said to me, "That was the boy you rescued."

CHAPTER 7

When we began the invasion of Sicily in 1943, we had of course the ultimate invasion of the Italian mainland in mind. After the conquest of Sicily I remarked to Lt-Cmdr Riley, who was in operational command of the whole of 30 commando, that I hoped that by the time of the Jewish New Year which was then but a month away, we would have got into Rome because there had been a magnificent synagogue there, though I had no idea whether after the German occupation there was any Jewish community left. During the fierce fighting in Salerno I was able to rescue Riley and a section of the commando who had been surrounded by the Germans. We were under heavy shelling and mortar fire and Riley's first remark to me was that I was unlikely to get to Rome in time for the New Year services. At that moment, as Riley and all his officers were wounded, I confessed I had more pressing worries.

However, providentially, events worked out differently and as I shall hereafter relate, I was to get to a shul for the "yomim tovim" though far away from Rome!!

After we had successfully held the Salerno salient, the Eighth Army, having occupied the southern part of Italy, advanced to within 15 miles of our lines. As the Germans withdrew from the intervening country, Lt Ogle and I went by jeep down the coast road to the front lines of the Eighth Army where we were closely interrogated about the situation at Salerno. From there we made our way to Taranto, as I was anxious to investigate the vast stories of enemy weapons in the Italian Naval stores at Boffaluto, part of the great Naval base of Taranto.

Whilst working there, after a short while I received an order to proceed forthwith to Malta for a Commanders' conference. This was in the week preceding the Jewish New Year. I immediately applied to Admiral Power, who was the Admiral in command in Taranto, but he explained that he had no means of conveying me to Malta rapidly. His suggestion was that I should proceed to the local airfield where I might find Royal Air Force planes which were flying on operations and would be returning to base in North Africa in the hope that one of them might take me to Malta on the way. Accordingly, I proceeded to the Airport where I found indeed a plane which was about to return to North Africa. The pilot said he was perfectly willing to help me get to Malta. In asking his assistance, I used the somewhat unfortunate phrase, "Will you drop me at Malta on your way to Africa?" He agreed to do so if I could assure him that he was authorised to do so. I therefore wrote out on a signal pad, "You are authorised to convey Commander Lincoln to Malta." I signed it with a squiggle and he gamely accepted this as authority. Accordingly, he sat me in the cockpit next to himself and we took off.

In the course of the journey, he asked me what I did in civilian life and I told him that I was in the Law. As we approached Malta itself, he called up one of his crew and asked him if they had any spare parachutes on board, telling me that their task had been to drop paratroops behind enemy lines to the North. With a perfectly straight face he said, "You did ask me to drop you at Malta," which I had to admit was true. When I expressed my horror, which by that time was perfectly visible, he retorted, "As a Lawyer, you should be careful of the words you use." However, he reassuringly told me that he would land, as he put it, "For a cup of tea."

Having at last safely reached Malta, I had to report aboard the Battleship Nelson, in which the Conference was to be held. On arriving on Quarterdeck, I was asked by the Officer of the Watch if I would wait for a few minutes to see the Ship's Captain, who would take me to the Admiral himself. Whilst we were pacing the Quarterdeck, we were approached by a Petty Officer who saluted the Officer of the Watch and asked for permission to speak to me. This Petty Officer turned out to be Petty Officer Goldstein whom I had known in London before the War and who had worked with me in a Society which was devoted to encouraging the young to observe the Sabbath. Goldstein's account of his arrival in the Battleship was fascinating. He had arrived to join the Ship on Friday evening, at that time in the rank of Able Seaman. As he was proceeding to the Crew's Quarters, he was greeted by a Chief Petty Officer who asked his name and then asked him if he was a Jew. When Goldstein said of course he was, the Chief Petty Officer greeted him with "Good Shabbas". It then transpired that the CPO had been raised in the East End of London and had earned a few pence as a youngster as a Shabbas Goy. A further point of interest was that Goldstein, who was the only Jew in a crew of 2000, had been assigned to listen in to German Submarine radio transmissions because of his knowledge of Yiddish, that being the nearest to any German speaking member of the crew.

All this had taken place two days before Rosh Hashana and the Conference itself finished on the day before the Festival. I immediately asked for and obtained three days leave to attend the local Synagogue. I was fortunate to find that although the local community was in the main a Sephardic community, the most prominent member was in fact, an Ashkenazi Jew, a member of the Devonport family called Joseph who had been associated with Naval supplies in Devonport and in Malta. Mr Joseph and his wife were most hospitable and delighted to see me because of our family connections through my mother's family in Devonport. I was therefore lucky enough to spend a very happy Rosh Hashana with them and in the local synagogue.

In the congregation at the synagogue, I was approached by an Italian Jew who had fled from the Fascist regime in Italy and had safely reached Malta. He told me that his sister and her husband were in hiding from the Nazis in Naples where they were being protected by a friendly Italian family. After Yom Tov, he gave me the address and asked me if we successfully occupied Naples, whether I would go to rescue them from their hiding place and in due course, he gave me some money to give to them. I promised him that I would do what I could.

On the day after Rosh Hashana, I learnt that a battalion of Palestinian Jews had been formed to fight with the British Army and was under the command of Major Wellesley Aron. They were encamped just outside Valleta and I was able to visit them and spend an evening in their company. Wellesley Aron himself was of course, a graduate of Cambridge University and we had worked together in Zionist work in England before the War. My knowledge of spoken Ivrit was, at that time, very limited and my attempt to speak to the assembled soldiers was greeted with very friendly mirth. Accordingly, I had to address them in English, which they understood perfectly well.

On leaving Malta, my hosts, Mr and Mrs Joseph, asked me to go back for Yom Kippur but I was unable to give them any assurance that this would be possible. As it turned out however, I was to benefit from great good fortune which was of advantage not only to myself, but to our Naval warfare. The way this came about was as follows: on my return to Taranto, I continued my investigation of the Italian magazine at Boffaluto and was able to discover carefully stored apparatus known to the Germans and Italians as YY II. This I immediately recognised as something which we had long been anxious to obtain. It was in fact, the method by which the Germans were able to counteract British acoustic mines. We had been searching for a long time to discover how this apparatus worked and this would enable us of course, to modify our own mines and make them impervious to German counter measures. Finding this apparatus and the method by which it worked was of utmost importance and I immediately signalled Captain Maitland Dougal at the Admiralty, the news of my discovery. The immediate reaction I had anticipated was that they wanted the apparatus itself, together with samples of the explosive charges which it used, dispatched by fast means from Malta to the Admiralty. It was essential, not only to send back the apparatus itself, but to have detailed drawings and photographs together with exact measurements, so that if by any mischance the original was lost, the machine itself could be reconstructed. It transpired that I could not get this important detailed work done in Taranto and so I was again sent back with it to Malta so that I could ensure that we had a complete description and analysis drawn up, together with the photographs and the original apparatus consigned to the Admiralty. This fortunate discovery meant that I had to return to Malta in time for Yom Kippur.

There was an interesting sequel, in that, on my return to Taranto after Yom Kippur, there was an acknowledgement from the Admiralty that they had received the apparatus, together with the specimen explosive charges by which it operated. The method of operation was that small explosive charges were dropped through a tube into the sea and were set off by electric contacts so as to create a staccato noise under the water. The size of the charges, of course, determined the frequency of sound thus created. The Admiralty Scientists requested that they could be supplied at the earliest possible moment with a minimum of 500 of the explosive charges for experimental purposes. I was very friendly with an Italian Naval Officer who had overall control of the magazine and with his assistance, I ascertained that there were nearly 2000 of the charges in question in the magazine. At this juncture, Admiral Power sent for me and said he had information that I was taking things from magazines without his knowledge or consent; and that as he was the Admiral in charge of the Italian Navy, it was my duty to get his consent to the removal of anything from the magazines. His words to me were, "All you have to do is ask me to get the Italian Navy to let you have what is required. They are most co-operative and will assist you in every way possible." I thereupon showed him the Admiralty signal requesting 500 specimen charges of the YY II. "Good," he said to me. "Give this signal to my Chief of Staff, Captain Eardley Wilmot, and he will see that it is appropriately dealt with." I had my doubts about the co-operative attitude of the

Italian Navy and so I went with my Italian friend to the magazine and took 500 of the explosive charges back with me to the hotel in which I was staying. I stored these explosive charges under my bed, leaving of course, 1500 of the charges still in the magazine. Two days later, Admiral Power sent for me and said, "I have the answer from the Italian Navy to the Admiralty's request." He showed me the Italian reply which was to the effect that they could not supply the Admiralty with the charges as they only had 30 of them. I was amused at this reply because I knew that there were at least 1500 charges still in the depot and furthermore, I was able to tell Admiral Power the true situation and confess to him that I already had the 500 charges which the Admiralty required, which he could dispatch to the Admiralty Scientists in compliance with their request. At first, I thought the Admiral was going to explode because quite clearly I had deliberately disobeyed his instructions by taking the 500 charges, but when he had my explanation of the position, he was quite pleased that he was able to comply with the Admiralty's signal in full, though he was somewhat dismayed by the reply that he had had from the Italians, whom he believed to be co-operative.

After the completion of my investigations at Taranto, I rejoined my Commando at Salerno for the next assignment which was the taking of the three islands in the Bay of Naples. The islands in question were Ischia, Procida and Capri. Although there was a large German Army of occupation in Naples itself, the islands were only lightly held in the main by the Italian Fascist troops but there was no fight left in them, as Italy had already surrendered.

The consequence was that we occupied these islands and I set up my Headquarters in the island of Ischia and without going into too much detail, ruled the three islands absolutely for some three weeks. The most exciting incidents of the period concerned the taking of Capri, but that is a longer story to be told elsewhere. At the end of three weeks, we received information which indicated that the Eighth Army under

Montgomery had advanced northwards sufficiently to launch an assault on Naples itself. Our Commando's role was to attack at the same time from Possillipo to the north of the city.

The city itself was completely in our hands after a day's fighting and I accordingly found myself in the position to undertake, as my first immediate mission, the rescue of the Jewish family whose brother I had met in Malta. Accordingly, accompanied by Staff Officer Lt Ogle, we went down the main street of the city. The address that I had been given was in an area known as Monte Calvario. I was totally unaware that this was a red light district. As we went down into the city, my enquiries of passers by were, of course, greeted with a certain amount of lewd smiles and enquiries as to whether I wanted a woman. From time to time, I would be told by one of the persons I stopped, "You do not want to go there, I can get you a better woman - my sister or my daughter etc." It was obvious that none of these people believed me when I said this was not the object of my enquiries, but I had to persist until I found the address I was seeking.

Ultimately we located the old and somewhat dilapidated house in which, according to my information, the family had been kept hidden by friendly Neapolitan families. On entering the house, we were directed to the top storey. The sound of our heavy footsteps in Army boots with which we were at the time equipped, echoing up the old wooden staircase, must have caused considerable alarm to the still terrified couple hiding in the garret. After all, it was only a matter of an hour at the most that the city had been liberated from German occupation, and this fact had not apparently been conveyed to the frightened family still in hiding. Naturally, in consequence when we hammered on the door of the garret, they were at first reluctant to open it and were highly suspicious of my calls to them in English, which could of course, have come from a Gestapo agent. Ultimately however, they accepted my assurances of having met the brother in Malta and we were able to get in and discuss the problems of their immediate freedom from what had been years of misery and despair.

So far as I was concerned, this represented a happy Mitzvah which was, I suppose a by-product of the War.

December 1943 saw me recalled to London.

My new task was to be the formation of another commando for the invasion of the continent which I was told was being planned in 1994. However events were to work out differently, for early in the new year we learned at the Admiralty that the US Navy had recovered intact six Japanese torpedoes and had not evaluated them. We immediately arranged with the US Naval attaché in London that I was to proceed to the USA to discover all we could about the speed range and explosive charge etc. of these weapons, as this information was of vital importance to our Pacific Fleet and the US Navy had not bothered to make the necessary investigations.

Accordingly I arranged for the US Army to fly me to America and for the torpedoes to be made available to me.

My arrival in Washington was shortly before Pesach for which festival I clearly had to make such arrangements as I could. First I had to take the explosive war heads to the magazine area at Indian Head Maryland. That done I despatched the bodies of the torpedoes to Newport Rhode Island where there was a torpedo testing range and as the Passover was imminent, the fact that there was a long established Jewish community there was for me a further factor of importance.

Meanwhile Admiral Pott, our attaché in Washington, gave me two days leave which enabled me to spend the Seder nights in New York where I had an emotional reunion with my parents who had gone there to escape the London bombing.

On arriving at Newport, I went to the City Hall to discover the address of the local Rabbi. I was greeted by the negro janitor who explained that he was a Baptist preacher and a personal friend of the Rabbi to whom he would gladly take me.

First however he insisted he must telephone him to say he was bringing round a Jewish commander from the British Navy.

When we arrived, the Rabbi welcomed me warmly and proceeded to explain that he was just studying a portion of the Talmud about the important duty to send away the mother bird before taking eggs from the nest. I knew the section well and shook him somewhat by saying, "Yes that is from Chulen," and proceeding to expound the Rabbinic commentary on it. He had not anticipated such from a Commander in the Royal Navy. We became firm friends and he generously invited me to eat with his family for the rest of Passover.

The Newport Jewish history is of particular fascination. The Synagogue was built by the Touro family of Sephardi immigrants about 1658 and the services still follow the Sephardi tradition, though the community is now predominantly Askenazi. The Rabbi must be a graduate of a Sephardic seminary.

The beautiful synagogue was visited by George Washington and still preserves many objects of Spanish origin. The original Sephardim came from the Spanish West Indies, where they had fled from the Inquisition.

PART 2

CHAPTER 8

1947

I left the Royal Navy in 1946 after having served an additional half year by volunteering to complete the mine clearance of the Baltic. I finally came back to practice at the Bar in October 1946, but found that practising conditions had changed very markedly in the intervening period. I .therefore decided to apply immediately for appointment to the rank of King's Counsel, relying in the main on the reputation I had established before 1939 and with the strong support of Lord du Parcq and the Hon Mr Justice Norman Birkett (as he then was). I was not very optimistic about my chances of getting this appointment. For one thing I was a Tory candidate for Parliament and the 1945 General Election had resulted in the return of a strong Labour Government. Nevertheless, Lord Jowitt, who was the Lord Chancellor, knew of me and of the strength of my pre-war practice and was not going to allow political considerations to interfere with judicial appointments. Accordingly, in March 1947 I found myself appointed King's Counsel. I was still under 40 years of age and was taking an active part in Jewish communal affairs, I was a Vice-President of the Zionist Federation and a Vice-President of the Jewish National Fund. More immediately active was my work as Chairman of the Political Committee of the World Jewish Congress. Although this was normally only for the British branch, as the Jewish communities throughout Europe had been largely slaughtered by the Nazis, the British branch of WJC was in effect, dealing with Europe as a whole. The result of this was that when in spring, a Peace Conference was assembled in Paris for negotiation of peace treaties between the Allied Powers and a number of minor countries that had joined with Germany against us in the War, such as Romania, Hungary, etc., the WJC was granted Associated status at the

Conference and I was appointed with Dr Stephen Barber as one of the representatives of the British section. Stephen Barber was, by training, a Czechoslovakian lawyer, a fluent linguist in French, German and English. The British delegation also comprised Alec Easterman who was the Executive Director of the British section and Dr Barou.

We accordingly found ourselves in Paris, negotiating with the various delegations to ensure that in any peace treaty, there should be an adequate safeguard against any recurrence of genocide such as the Holocaust. It is right to say that in our efforts to obtain this form of international guarantee for the settlement of European affairs, we had the fullest support of the British Foreign Office representatives. We also had strong support from unexpected sources, because we found that the Ethiopian Delegation representing the then Emperor Haile Selase was being advised by an outstanding Jewish lawyer, namely Norman Bentwich who had been a Law Officer in the British Mandatory Government in Palestine.

With all this plethora of legal advice, a satisfactory formulation and the type of guarantee we required was soon arrived at.

Once the negotiations in Paris were satisfactorily completed and the Treaties accepted in their final form, there were other immediate tasks which required urgent attention on the Continent of Europe. It must be borne in mind that the Concentration Camps had only been liberated shortly before these events and although we were now more that a year after the cessation of hostilities, there were still many thousands of homeless refugees wandering about Europe, their future unsettled. Accordingly, Dr Stephen Barber and myself undertook negotiations with a view to tackling the problem. These negotiations had a series of options which had to be explored. The obvious solution would have been free and unrestricted immigration to Palestine, but this avenue was firmly closed by the restrictions still being imposed by the Mandatory Government. It is true that as a matter of historical fact, a considerable breach in the official policy was made by the illegal immigration boats which were organised under the heading of "Aliyah Beth". However, this was not a matter with which we could deal immediately, although I was able to approach the French Navy in Paris on a strictly confidential basis with a request that they should not interfere with "Aliyah Beth" ships leaving Marseilles or other Mediterranean Ports. Fortunately, I had been co-operating during the War with an Admiral of the Free French Navy, Admiral Louis Khan, who was of a distinguished French Jewish family. His story was a remarkable one - on the surrender of France, the Vichy Government had ordered his arrest. He had, however, been able to escape from prison because of the attitude of sympathetic Prison Officers who were anti-Nazi and respected him and his high rank in the French Navy. With the help of such sympathisers, he had been able to escape through Spain and finally reached Gibraltar from where he was enabled by the British Navy to join the Free French Forces in England. When, therefore, I discussed the refugee situation with him at the Ministry of Marine in Paris, it was not difficult to persuade him to turn a blind eye to the refugee ships in the Mediterranean.

Dr Barber and I then proceeded to Luxembourg where we were granted an interview with the Prime Minister. We pointed out to him that we were able to get permits in limited numbers for refugees to go to Palestine and to the United States. These had to be spread over a period of months ahead. We therefore sought from him the grant of immigration visas to Luxembourg of two types - one class clearly was visas for permanent residence and the other type was for visas for temporary residence of a transit nature, on the basis that the temporary visa holder would ultimately proceed onwards to some other country which was ready to grant permanent residential status. After some discussion, it transpired that there were certain categories of professionals which were in particular shortage in Luxembourg. One was doctors and the other was tailors - both of which we were happy to supply from our refugee list. The Prime Minister also agreed that we could have several thousand permits for transits who would ultimately have to proceed onwards. We had the satisfaction of knowing, however, that as a result of this visit, upwards of another ten thousand refugees had been immediately cared for.

When we began our negotiations with the Prime Minister, Dr Barber and I felt that it would be courteous to him to speak in French, and accordingly, we began our discussions in that language. In Luxembourg itself, French, German and Luxemborgoise are the common languages. However, after a short discussion, we reached a moment when I found myself lost for a word and asked Dr Barber for the French equivalent. With a laugh, the Prime Minister intervened making it quite clear that he understood English perfectly well. I then said to him, "Sir, it is quite clear that you speak English and understand it. Would you think us discourteous if we speak in English?" His reply was, "You forget that I have been spending the War years in exile with our Royal Family in Scotland." We were then able to conclude our successful discussions in shorter time and certainly in a language which it was easier for me to handle.

The year was to hold many more outstanding events from my point of view. During the summer, I decided to take the whole family to Gibraltar to spend a holiday with my brother who was serving as a regular Army Officer and was a Major in the Royal Engineers. He was enjoying the privilege of having an official residence there and had his wife and children with him. There were at that time, severe restrictions on allowances and currency for foreign travel, restricting each traveller to a limit of £25 - however long the holiday. It was obviously vital to be able to take advantage of the free hospitality which my brother was able to offer.

During the six weeks that we spent in Gibraltar, the three ships of the Exodus incident arrived in the Harbour. The story of these three ships was that they had left Hamburg in Germany packed with Jewish refugees who wanted to enter Palestine. The ships sailed quite openly but the British Government, represented by Ernest Bevin, as Foreign Secretary, publicly announced that under no circumstances would these refugees be permitted to enter Palestine. The policy of the British Government up to that moment had been that when an illegal immigrant ship was stopped by the Royal Navy, the passengers had been landed at Haifa and then transferred to Famagusta in Cyprus where a large internment camp for Jewish refugees was established. Ernest Bevin, however, decided that he would make a demonstration of his opposition to Jewish immigration into Palestine by decreeing an especially draconian treatment for these three refugee ships. He ordered that when the ships arrived in Palestinian waters, they were to be turned round and ordered back to Hamburg. When one considers the extent of the Holocaust and the persecution that the Jews received in Nazi Germany, there was a special flavour of refined cruelty in ordering that these ships should take their refugee passengers back to Germany. It was in the course of this return journey that the three ships put into Gibraltar Harbour, where they were made to anchor near the off shore mole and were heavily guarded by Naval and Police patrol boats. In conforming with the policy of the London Government, the Gibraltarian authorities forbade any contact with the ships. At that time, the Leader of the Gibraltar Jewish Community was the Hon David Benaim. His general attitude was that the comparatively small Jewish community of Gibraltar must do everything possible to demonstrate their loyalty to Great Britain and he adopted an avowedly anti Zionist attitude, thinking that thereby he was pursuing a policy parallel to that of the British Foreign Office. His views on this matter were not shared by all the members of the local Jewish community, but his attitude was such that it was impossible to get the official organs of the community to take any action towards communicating with the refugees in the ships or offering them any help.

When my brother and I discovered that this was to be the official policy of the community, we decided that we would try to get the help of those members of the community who were willing, even unofficially, to do something. The first requirement, obviously, was to get Government permission to contact the refugees themselves, to discover what their immediate needs were. Accordingly, my brother as a local Army Officer and myself a visiting King's Counsel, sought and obtained an interview with the Colonial Secretary. His initial attitude was very hostile. His opening gambit was, "How dare you hope to give any assistance to these people who are Britain's enemies?" Gently but firmly I pointed out that in no sense of the word could these helpless and desperate refugees be described as enemies of Britain. Ultimately, we convinced him that on grounds of pure humanity, as well as Christian charity, some assistance and comfort might be legitimately given. He, however, demanded an assurance that no arms or weapons of any kind would be supplied. This was an assurance that we were readily able to give and having received permission, we proceeded with the help of several of the local Jewish community, to collect supplies of milk, food stuffs and cigarettes. The next task was to organise transport of supplies to the Port for conveyance to the ships. A fleet of lorries was organised by Mr Samuel Marrache and these were loaded and with official permission, passed through the docks. We were happy to receive emotional letters of thanks from the ships who also sent greetings for the approaching New Year.

It is interesting perhaps to round off the story by subsequent events. When the ships ultimately reached Hamburg, their arrival coincided with the subsequent developments at the United Nations and the declaration by Ernest Bevin that Great Britain was relinquishing the Mandate. The fact that a Jewish State was about to come into existence meant that the refugees did not disembark at Hamburg and the ships immediately set sail once more for Palestine.

CHAPTER 9

Shortly after my return from Gibraltar, an urgent meeting was held in London. It was a secret meeting of the Zionist chief executives to consider the crisis situation that had arisen in Palestine. Relations between the Mandatory authorities and the Jewish Agency were at their nadir. In desperation, the High Commissioner and his civil servants were threatening the Yishuv and the Agency leaders with a variety of sanctions if there was no cessation of Irgun or Lehi terrorism and further if the Haganah did not arrest or hand over the leaders of those groups.

The meeting was summoned by Halevy, the national chairman of the Zionist Federation, and was attended by Teddy Kolleck and Abba Eban among others. After much discussion, they asked me if I would agree to go out to Palestine to see if something practical could be achieved by friendly discussion. This I agreed to do subject to the stipulation that I should have some letter or other document showing that my mission had at least the tacit blessing of the Colonial Office. This I duly received and armed with it, I proceeded to Palestine and there made contact with those at the High Commission who were willing to assist in an endeavour to re-establish good relations. At first things looked hopeful. I had found one of the senior members of the government secretariat whose brother was a fellow QC and friend of mine at the Bar in London. He took an absolutely unbiased approach and was as helpful as he could be. But then suddenly one Saturday there was a pitched battle in Jerusalem after the Goldsmith Officers' Club was blown up with the loss of several lives. At the time of this outrage, I was actually a guest in the home of a senior civil servant and the Officers' Club was between myself and my hotel. As a curfew was immediately imposed, the soldiers would not at first allow me to pass their lines and made me go under escort to their HQ post to have my Colonial pass verified.

Not surprisingly, this severe outbreak of terrorist activity caused Gen Gale, who commanded the army in the country, to lose patience and martial law was imposed upon the Yishuv. This was a most serious and draconian measure, which brought the whole economy to an immediate standstill. In one way it indicated that there was a total failure of ordered government. All banks were closed and communications severed. I found myself in a unique position, as with my pass I could travel freely in my car around the country. I was therefore frequently asked to carry out missions as a favour to those who were, as it were, virtually immobilised. I resolved that I would not abuse my privileged pass by in any way doing anything that was against official policy. When therefore I was asked by the Chief Rabbi Hertzog if I would rescue his Yeshiva students by bringing money in my car from Tel Aviv to Jerusalem, I sought the express permission of Gen Gale himself to comply. As it was a humanitarian gesture and not a normal commercial transaction he readily assented.

Shortly after, I was asked to undertake an unusual task of a more serious nature. The background story was a reflection of the post-war situation in the Middle East. When the British forces left the desert battlefields of North Africa they left on Egyptian territory vast quantities of war material of all kinds - innumerable partially damaged vehicles, tanks, jeeps personnel carriers etc. There was even a complete power station as well as miles of barbed wire. The whole area was a scrap merchant's dream and was of great value. In fact an offer of £20 million was accepted by the British government. Then the Egyptian government refused an export permit for any of the equipment. An Egyptian company was then formed in which the King and his Prime Minister were financially interested and a small offer was made to Britain for the material. As it was impossible to remove anything without official permission, this company necessarily acquired it all.

Among the scrap, there were hundreds of miles of water pipes. These were urgently required in the Yishuv to supply new Kibbutzim especially in the Negev. A Tel Aviv company therefore negotiated the purchase of some 180 miles of these pipes for the use of the JNF in developing new colonies. Part payment by way of deposit had been made before martial law was imposed. But now a demand was being made for completion of the deal forthwith. Somehow or other, a banker's draft had to get to Cairo or the deal would fail. The Tel Aviv company therefore offered to charter an Al Misr plane of the Egyptian Air Lines to take me to Cairo and bring me back. Again I went to see the General and put the case to him. In one sense this was a commercial transaction, but there was also the humanitarian side of an essential water supply to the new colonies. There was the not inconsiderable detail that the King of Egypt was anxious to see the rest of the money paid over. Consent was therefore given and in due course the chartered plane stood waiting for me at Lod airport. On arrival at Cairo, I was met and escorted to Sheperds Hotel where I was invited to dine with a charming gentleman who was the director of the vendor company and who had ready the receipted documents and export licence for the pipes. While we were at dinner, there was a sudden disturbance as the King himself arrived and sat at an adjoining table to see that the banker's draft was handed over. He was surrounded by a large bodyguard and other guards stood at the restaurant doors and in the corridors outside. When they all left, I counted more than 20 armed guards as he went to his car.

My plane had waited for me and I returned to Lod as quickly as possible with my precious documents, happy to be back safely.

It was a pleasant surprise that the contract was promptly honoured and the pipes were speedily delivered. Steps were immediately taken to ensure their use for the Kibbutzim. I was told that at Ruhamma in the northern Negev, trenches were to be dug for the pipeline and that volunteer parties of foreign visitors were vying for the "honour" of doing a spell of digging to help out the Kibbutzniks. Somewhat rashly in a burst of unthinking enthusiasm, I agreed to volunteer for trench digging mainly because I wanted to see "my pipes" doing their job. I had not realised what digging under that sun entailed, but I rapidly learnt as did the others and after a back breaking spell we were glad to hand over our spades to their rightful owners. Still it was a novel experience to see new Kibbutzim taking shape with elaborate defences as the first task. It was immediately apparent how vitally essential the pipes were as a prelude to the setting up of any new settlement and how gigantic was the task of allocating and installing them to become part of a country-wide grid.

CHAPTER 10

During the period of martial law, there was one incident that was of a particular emotional impact. It arose in this way. During the time that I had been number one of the investigation section into mines and underwater weapons at the Admiralty from 1940 to 1942, there were times at which different Senior Captains held the office of Director of Torpedoes and Mining of which department my investigation section was a subsidiary section. At one time, the Director was a Captain de Salis, who was a fervent Roman Catholic. His brother, Colonel de Salis, was in fact, the British Ambassador to the Vatican. This Captain de Salis was openly and avowedly, violently anti-semitic. To my horror, he made no secret of his views in that respect. This was an attitude which I am happy to say I hardly ever encountered in the Royal Navy. The vast majority of Senior Officers were willing and anxious to treat you as an individual Officer without regard to any question of religion; de Salis, however, was so violent in his views that when I was recommended for a second mention in Despatches for commando operations, he passed on the recommendation to the Honours and Awards committee, but when it was accepted he sent for me and said that had he realised I was a Jew, he would never have made the recommendation. This was naturally very hurtful and I was horrified to hear such a remark from a Senior Naval Officer. However, when martial law was declared in Palestine, I heard that the Officer commanding Naval forces off that coast was none other than this same Captain de Salis. I accordingly took the opportunity to go to his Headquarters, not in any spirit of revenge but on the contrary, to sound out his attitude with the object of hoping that he might, in the intervening years, have modified his extreme views.

Martial law had been proclaimed of course, because of the extremist acts of the terrorist organisations which had committed a series of outrageous attacks on civilian as well as military targets. The Civil Service had been hit by the blowing up of the King David Hotel in Jerusalem and the Goldsmith Officers' Club had been blown up, causing a number of casualties amongst the Army Officers there. As a result of this sort of activity, it was natural that the Navy Headquarters in Haifa were very heavily protected by barbed wire and sandbag emplacements. In order to gain entrance, I had to show my Colonial Office pass and satisfy the Security Officers as to my personal trustworthiness. At the very heart of this heavily fortified base, I found Captain de Salis who exhibited quite clearly every sign of terror. His pallor was deathly white and when I came into his room, he greeted me with an almost hysterical shout of, "Tell your Jews to call off these terror attacks forthwith." I pointed out to him that I had no power over these terrorist organisations, but was there in Palestine for the very purpose of trying hard to improve relations between the Jewish authorities and the Mandatory Government.

De Salis of course, was mainly concerned with the Naval operations of patrolling destroyers to intercept and divert illegal immigrant ships. There were so many of these small illegal immigrant vessels that some were bound to get through and the number was causing considerable embarrassment. Of course, the whole operation of this illegal immigration resulted from the overwhelming compulsion of the combination of the vast numbers of Jewish refugees from the German Concentration Camps and forced labour centres, who were wandering Europe without homes to which they could return - plus the fact that the Labour Government under the influence of Ernest Bevin had decreed that there should be no further legal immigration into Palestine. In the vain effort to stem the pressing flood of illegal immigration, British destroyers were used to patrol the Eastern Mediterranean and when they caught an illegal ship, to divert it to Haifa Harbour. Once there, the illegal immigrants were taken into custody and transferred to a vast camp which had been created at Famagusta in Cyprus. De Salis then quite viciously said, "This illegal immigration policy must be stopped and you," pointing his finger at me, "must tell your Jews to stop it, otherwise," said he, "I shall give orders that future illegal ships are to be torpedoed and we shall not bother to rescue the criminals." I pointed out to him as calmly as I could, that the Mandate had been granted to Britain on the express purpose of implementing the Balfour Declaration, which called for the creation of a Jewish National Home in Palestine and that therefore, an absolute prohibition of legal immigration could not possibly be justified from the legal point of view. I also pointed out to him, that it must be apparent to him that no British destroyer would torpedo a ship filled with homeless immigrants and leave them to drown and he must know it. On this note we had to part. I must confess that I had a certain amount of personal satisfaction at seeing him with his violent prejudices, cowering behind a mass of sandbags and barbed wire.

The year 1947 was to contain yet other vital and exciting moments. Towards the end of November, I sat with a number of leaders of the British Zionist Movement to listen to the radio reports of the Debate in the United Nations Assembly which was to decide what was to happen in Palestine. It had become quite apparent from my own experiences there, that the Government of the country had fallen into complete chaos and indeed, the imposition of martial law had not resulted in resolving in any way, the difficulties of the Mandatory administration. On the one hand, the Arabs were in open insurrection and the British Government were under the most intense international pressure at their refusal to permit legal immigration as a possible solution to the intolerable refugee problem. As a result of all these difficulties, it had become apparent that lawful satisfactory Government had become impossible. Ernest Bevin, the British Foreign Secretary, was never personally favourably disposed towards Jews. He, together with the Webbs, who became Lord and Lady Passfield, had been for some considerable while openly anti-semitic. When, therefore, Britain was faced with the immense problems of the Palestinian situation, Bevin announced that they would give up the Mandate and simply leave the country on the basis that from the British point of view, the Arabs and Jews could settle the problems between themselves. The buck therefore was placed firmly in the hands of the United Nations and a decision had to be taken as to what was to happen to the country. A plan had been drawn up for the division of the country into Jewish areas and Arab areas. It was therefore a vital decision which was to be made by the Assembly of the United Nations as to whether this scheme should be implemented. Acceptance required a two thirds vote in favour. Consequently, we listened anxiously to the debate and to the counting of the votes. One country after another declared itself and anxiously we awaited the outcome. Finally, came the vote of Peru which gave the necessary majority and meant that at long last, after some two thousand years of waiting, a Jewish state was to be set up. Whilst the concept itself gave the greatest cause for rejoicing, our pleasure nevertheless was restricted by the realisation that the areas allotted to the proposed Jewish state were extremely small. Because of this limitation, there was in some Jewish quarters hesitation about acceptance of the decision.

The decision having been taken at the end of November, a large celebratory meeting was organised by the Zionist Organisation to be held at the Lyceum Theatre in London in December. The principal speaker at this meeting was Doctor Chaim Weizman who had been recognised for many years as the leader of world Zionism. As a Vice-President of the Zionist Federation, I was on the platform at this meeting and was designated to propose the vote of thanks to Doctor Weizman after his speech. I was surprised and concerned that his speech consisted in the main of an earnest plea to the Jews of the world to reject the Resolution of the United Nations on the ground that the area allocated for the proposed Jewish State was ludicrously small and in his view, not viable from the economic point of view. I noted in his speech what might have been called the keynote theme "we have waited 2000 years for a State, and we can now wait for a further period before rushing in with an acceptance". In my own speech, I had the temerity to oppose this attitude vigorously. I spoke with some passion because I had been face to face with the refugee problem in Europe and I ventured to make the somewhat impudent remark that, "It is only the old who can wait, the young cannot." In venturing to oppose so eminent a personage, I had well in mind my own feeling that once a Jewish State was established, it would not long be restricted to the minute area allocated, but would either by diplomacy or force of arms, acquire a fully viable area. This obviously was not a point of view that it would have been wise to express publicly, but in my own mind, it formed the foundation for justifying the strongest possible advocacy for acceptance of the UN Resolution. Fortunately, as history records, Ben Gurion and Shertok, the leaders of the Jewish Agency, had much the same point of view and by the end of December were taking active steps to set up the nucleus of a projected Government infrastructure. Mr Shertok, who was the Agency's Foreign Affairs Minister, was frequently in London at that time with two assistants, Abba Eban and Teddy Kolleck, both of them young men of my own age with whom I had a close acquaintance. I was also at that time active in research work for the Royal Institute of International Affairs, Chatham House, where I had been working on research together with Commander Stephen King-Hall from years before the War began. I was also, of course, active as Chairman of the World Jewish Congress, Europe Committee, and with the combination of all these contacts, I had frequent occasions for discussions with Shertok and his staff. I thus learned that the plans of the Jewish Agency in relation to projected arms forces were concentrated on the build-up of an Army based of course, on the Haganah and the creation of an Air Force, in relation to which, help was being sought from supporters in the United States. It was clear from my discussions that no-one had contemplated the formation of a Navy. To my mind, the long coastline of Palestine called urgently for the creation of a Naval force. Unfortunately, the value of Naval forces is not generally understood by the lay world. The public imagination is always fired by the recollection of great Naval battles and victories - Trafalgar, Jutland, the sinking of the Bismark and the battle of the River Plate are all ingrained in the popular concept of the role of the Navy. But there are other vital tasks for which a Naval capacity is essential. The escorting of supply ships and the ability to escort troop carrying ships are but two of these vital functions. I made representations accordingly to Shertok, who asked me to prepare a detailed memorandum for the consideration of Ben Gurion and the Jewish Agency.

Accordingly, I set out my arguments in favour of a Navy and my proposals for its use. I passed my memorandum to Shertok, who in early January 1948 passed it on to Ben Gurion. As I afterwards discovered, Ben Gurion himself and many of the leaders of the Agency, having come from mid European origins, had no knowledge of the sea or any concept of all the functions a Navy could perform. Ben Gurion himself expressed the view that in the modern world, the only things that counted were an Army backed by air power, and that there was no room or requirement for a Naval force. My memorandum argued forcibly against this narrow, and in my opinion, uninformed point of view. As I afterwards discovered, Ben Gurion passed my memorandum to a non-Jewish Naval Officer, one Captain Miller who was the principal instructor in Navigation and Seamanship at the Haifa Maritime School which had been set up some time before by the activities of the Palestine Maritime League. I had been the Chairman of the British section of this League. There was also another Maritime School in Palestine supported by a movement called Zebulun which was largely the child of Mrs Henrietta Diamond who had been its Chairman and Founder in England. Both these Maritime Schools had been concerned with producing seamen and officers for merchant ships and there was in existence, a small Merchant Navy line known as the Zim Line which had been founded by the Borchardt family who had originally been owners of a company of tugs in Hamburg. Some of the graduates of these Maritime Schools had come to England and had gone to Italy to obtain further training for Masters Tickets and there was thus a nucleus of Naval personnel trained in navigation and seamanship. Captain Miller, to whom my memorandum was submitted, informed Ben Gurion that he completely endorsed my arguments and strongly supported the formation of the Navy. The question was apparently bandied about between one source and another and it was not until March 1948 that a final decision was taken that in addition to the Army and Air Force, there should be a Navy.

CHAPTER 11

In my memorandum or paper to Ben Gurion on the need for a Navy, I had stressed certain functions. One was the utility of a naval force for the easy movement of troops from one part of the coast to another, which I foresaw would provide a mobility which could be of great advantage in any military operations. Another priority was the necessity to escort supply ships and to protect the many immigrant ships which were still at that stage on their way to Palestine. There was also the need to intercept any enemy vessels which might approach our coasts or harbours, though this might call for a sizeable armoured fleet with effective attacking weapons.

As I have previously stated, Ben Gurion sought an authoritative non-Jewish opinion on my memorandum from Capt. Miller, who had been a British Naval Officer and was the director of the Haifa Maritime School. His strong endorsement of my views was in the hands of Ben Gurion by early February, but the formation of a navy did not assume for Ben Gurion or his advisers any special or immediate importance. There had been an intimation from the British Government that they would be giving up the administration by mid May so there was a target date by which everything had to be in place. There were many vital decisions which had to be taken and these were postponed for a meeting of the Actions Committee of the Jewish Agency which was called for March. At that meeting, a final decision as to the composition of the Armed Forces was made and this included an agreement that a Navy should be formed.

Accordingly, following this meeting, Professor Selig Brodetsky the British representative returned to London accompanied by Mr Shragai. They sent for me and said they were authorised to request me to proceed forthwith to Palestine to form the Navy. At the same time they emphasised that this was on a voluntary basis as I had anticipated.

The first and immediate problem was how to get to Palestine. All airlines had already withdrawn their air services because there had been an outbreak of Arab violence which had made the principal airfield at Lod unusable. After some discussion with Lavy Bakstansky, the Executive Director of the British Zionist Federation, I was furnished with the sum of £80 and an air ticket to Cyprus. It was realised of course, that Cyprus was still some distance away from Palestine, but I was assured that some means would be found through Haganah agents in Cyprus to get me to Palestine. Accordingly, I flew to Cyprus and as I left the plane, I was approached by a Cypriot who told me his name was Georgiades which is a common name in Cyprus, rather like saying in England, "My name is Mr Smith." Georgiades told me that he was secretly an agent for the Haganah and had made arrangements to accommodate me in a local hotel for, hopefully, only a few days until he could arrange my onward travel. His instructions to me were, that in the hotel bar I would meet a number - about 15 or 20 - of Britishers who each owned a private plane and who were making a living by flying to the troubled spots of the world and offering their services. "Have a drink with them," he said, "and try and arrange for one of them to fly you over to the airfield at Haifa." That evening in the bar, I had a very friendly meeting with the air mercenaries, but one and all they declined to undertake the mission that I was seeking because they said the insurance companies who covered their planes had stated that the cover would be withdrawn if they flew to Palestine at that juncture. The next morning, I reported this sad outcome to Georgiades who then said he had an alternative way in mind, which was to smuggle me into the refugee camp that had been established at Famagusta for the vast number of Aliyah Beth refugees who had been intercepted by the British Naval forces. In order to relieve pressure on the accommodation and resources of the Camp, the British

Government was sending a small number of immigrants by sea at frequent intervals to Haifa and it was thought that I could be got on to one of these boats. I was not particularly pleased at this prospect, mainly because it meant a delay of several days and by this time it was early April. However, I had to accept this suggestion as being the best that the Agent thought could be done. But later that day Georgiades appeared excitedly at the hotel. His news was that a plane which belonged to King Abdullah of Trans Jordan would be flying in to Cyprus Airport at dawn the following morning, bringing several officials of the Shell Oil Company. The pilot of the plane was British, a certain Captain X. He would be flying the plane back to Trans Jordan empty and, said Georgiades, "If you are willing to pay him what he asks, he might land you at Haifa on his way back to Trans Jordan." As a result of this, I waited for the plane at dawn the following morning and followed Captain X into the RAF Mess, where we had a short discussion. He said he was quite willing to take the risk of landing at Haifa on his return journey and would take me for £80, to be paid in cash before we left. This sum I had but I was not willing or anxious to part with the whole of it. Nevertheless, I agreed with the Captain that I would meet him at the airport a little later that day and pay him. I then went back to the hotel where I had met a British journalist, Patrick O'Donovan who had been sent out by The Observer to report on the latest news in the Middle East and who was as anxious as I was to get to Palestine. I explained the situation to him and he agreed to pay £40 towards the cost. When all was arranged, Georgiades said that there was a young Jew called Herman who had come from Canada and was anxious to get to Palestine in order to join the Haganah and thought that perhaps we could give him a lift in the plane. There was also a young lady, whose married name I have forgotten, but whose first name was Pamela. She was a member of a distinguished Anglo-Jewish family of my acquaintance and her single name had been Wigoder. Her husband was already enrolled in the Haganah, for she had been married and living in Palestine for some little while and she was at that moment heavily pregnant and anxious to rejoin her husband. Georgiades thought we might offer both of these people accommodation in the plane and to this Captain X agreed.

The next worry of course, was to discover which Forces were in control of the Haifa Airfield. Georgiades assured me that it was safely in Haganah control but this did not end my anxiety because the plane in which we were going to fly was painted in Arab colours and I was anxious that the Haganah should be fully apprised of our coming to avoid the chance of a hostile reception. Georgiades assured me that he was in radio contact with the Haganah who would be fully advised of the circumstances. In fact they were never informed. We accordingly took off and in due course, arrived over Haifa Airfield which appeared to be little more than a grassy strip with no apparent control tower, but an airsock lazily flapping at one end of the field. The plane was a Piper Cub, a twin winged single engine plane of the type which was largely used for training in the British forces. We landed without incident and Captain X who was obviously not anxious to be captured by the Haganah, hustled us out into the middle of the field so that he could immediately take off again for his journey to Amman. We all trudged with our luggage across the deserted Airfield to the nearest road. To our surprise, we had not been challenged by any armed patrol on either side. We had not gone far along the road to Haifa when we met a Haganah Patrol to whom we had to give an account of ourselves. The Officer in charge of this Patrol was an American Jew who had volunteered for service with the Haganah. He of course challenged us in Hebrew but it was not difficult to hear the Yankee twang in his Hebrew and so I was able to explain the situation to him in English. He immediately said he would arrange for transport for us all to Haifa and report our arrival to the HQ in Haifa. When I arrived in Haifa itself, I booked into a hotel and to my pleasant surprise, was told by the hotel proprietor that he had to report my arrival to the local Haganah Headquarters, as all hotels had been alerted to look out for Commander Lincoln. From that moment, I was taken in charge by the Haganah who said that the road from Haifa to Tel Aviv was not yet open as intruding Arab forces were blocking it at one point. However, that night a concerted attack preceded by a mortar bombardment from Ahusa successfully dislodged the Arab force so that my jeep was able to take me down the road to Ben Gurion's Headquarters the next morning.

These Headquarters had been set up in a building known as the Beth Adom and upon my arrival, I was greeted by Ruben Shiloah who immediately showed me in to Ben Gurion. Ben Gurion then told me that he had designated a leading member of the Histatadruth (the equivalent of the TUC) to assist with the appointment of personnel and one Avrum Ben Zakkai, who was a qualified sailor to take charge of the service side. I did not immediately appreciate the point about a Histatadruth representative until I was later to become more acquainted with the devious nature of politics inside the State Organisation that was being set up. No secret was made of the fact that the Histatadruth representative had no more maritime experience than looking after the carp ponds in his Kibbutz. He, however, proved fully co-operative on the labour side and in fact, had already mobilised some thousand men - 800 of whom were said to have served in the Royal Navy. They undoubtedly had, but when I came to investigate, I found that they had served in stores or chart indexing and generally in shore-based jobs and not one of them could be described as a sailor.

The next task was to assemble all these Naval personnel together in a camp at Haifa. Here we began to experience our first problem, namely indiscipline. This was a fault that was quite rife throughout even the Haganah itself and the problem was to surface in an acute form once the new State was declared. However, the end of the Mandate was still a month away or more and there was much preparatory work required. In addition to finding men, we had of course to find ships. In a section of Haifa Harbour, 22 ships which had been captured as Aliya Beth ships had been segregated after seizure by the Royal Navy. These interned ships varied considerably in type and size and two of them were ex-Royal Canadian Navy frigates and one was an ex-American Coast Guard ice-breaking patrol vessel. This particular ship was the largest of all, being about 2,500 tons and had the virtue of having a reinforced hull of heavy armour plating which would obviously make it useful in case of conflict. All these ships had lain idle for some time and it was essential to get their machinery into working order. We were faced with the obstacle that the British Forces were pursuing what they regarded as a policy of strict neutrality as between the Arabs and Jews. In practice this unfortunately worked out as the disarming of Haganah and other Service personnel and it was clearly going to be impossible to get the consent of the Authorities for Naval personnel to take over the 22 ships. However, in order to keep the Harbour working commercially, the Marines who patrolled the Harbour were forced to admit quite freely all authorised dock workers. Our Histatadruth man therefore obtained, for each of us, a membership card of the Histatadruth and we entered the Harbour to work on these ships as authorised dock workers. We had of course, at all times, the fullest co-operation from Aba Kushi who was the Mayor of Haifa and the Civic Authorities.

The first opportunity for what might be called "a Naval operation" occurred in early May. The military situation at that time was that Jaffa, which was still of course an Arab city, was under heavy attack from a Jewish force which consisted of Haganah Units and separately organised and commanded units of the Irgun Zvi Leumi. Despite strenuous efforts by Ben Gurion and his advisers, the Irgun insisted at this stage in maintaining this separate military organisation who would co-operate with the Haganah but not consent to a unified command. The fighting for Jaffa was very heavy, but gradually the Arab resistance was being borne down and defeated. When therefore, by about the beginning of May it became apparent that Jaffa would be overrun and conquered, the Arabs appealed to the British Authorities because they said they feared for their safety after the city was occupied. Accordingly, the British Military placed a substantial force in position between the contending sides. A conference was then called which met in Tel Aviv in which it was agreed that the Arabs would surrender the city under certain safeguards. The occupation by Jewish Forces was to take place in stages - the British Military arranged that at different times and dates, the positions would be evacuated by them and taken over in an orderly fashion by the Jewish Forces. Once this surrender by land had been arranged, Ben Gurion sent for me and said, "I want you to arrange for a Naval Force to occupy the Jaffa Port and in particular, I want a Naval patrol to operate outside the Port, because," he said, "the Arabs will attempt to evacuate a large part of their military material by sea." In the Port of Jaffa at that time, there was a large number of Arab Dhows and the task given to me was to organise patrol vessels which would stop and search the Dhows as they left the Port. I asked Ben Gurion what flag our patrol vessels should fly and he said, "The Jewish flag, of course." I pointed out to him that we did not as yet have a State, and to send armed men to seize cargoes from the Dhows, constituted in international law, an act of piracy. The serious side to this, as I saw it, was that British destroyers which were in constant patrol along the coast, might lawfully arrest our crews and might, if so minded, execute them as they were entitled to do under international law. Ben Gurion thought that the risk was negligible and should be taken.

We thereupon mustered two or three fishing boats, each of which carried ten men, armed them with sten guns and fitted them out with large Jewish flags and radio and instructed them to stop all Dhows leaving Jaffa and search them and confiscate anything in the way of military material. I set up a temporary Admiralty in the San Remo Hotel, an old hotel on the outskirts of Tel Aviv, where we installed a radio set so that we could keep in constant communication with our patrolling ships. From the roof of the Hotel, it was perfectly possible to have a clear view of the ships themselves.

One by one, the Dhows duly emerged from Jaffa Harbour and were stopped and searched. The search in fact proved most successful, so that our patrol vessels had to return rapidly and frequently to Tel Aviv Harbour with hundreds of rifles and thousands of rounds of ammunition.

During the course of this operation, a large Royal Naval flotilla, consisting of two cruisers and a number of destroyers, appeared off the coast. It was in fact, although I did not know it at the time, the Naval flotilla which had been designated to enter Haifa Harbour and evacuate the High Commissioner and his staff which would signal the end of the Mandate. For a few moments, my heart stood still as I feared the destroyers would arrest my little patrol boats, but to my great relief, they made no attempt to interfere.

When finally my eighty sailors entered and occupied Jaffa Harbour, we were presented with a surprise gift. There, we found two absolutely modern gun boats which had been used by the British Customs for purposes of interception. These small and fast vessels were in practically perfect condition, except that on leaving, their Officers had put the machinery out of action by removing some vital parts. We therefore towed the two MGB's back to Tel Aviv where in a very short time, our engineers were able to repair the machinery so that my little Navy was at last beginning to take shape.

On the 14th May, Friday evening on the eve of the Sabbath, the State of Israel was declared. The next morning at dawn, I was awakened by the roar of Egyptian Spitfire planes which were dive bombing the small Harbour at Tel Aviv. I must confess that having myself experienced the German blitz on London, I was concerned as to whether air attack might result in something of a civilian panic. In fact, it was quite the reverse. On going out on the balcony in my hotel to see what the Egyptian planes were doing, I could see that people from surrounding blocks of flats were out on their balconies vainly shaking their fists at the Egyptian bombers and not showing the slightest signs of panic. There was of course, a woeful shortage in anything of the way of anti-aircraft protection. I immediately went to the Beth Adom to see Ben Gurion who even at that early hour, was already at work in his office. When I saw him, I said, "Well Prime Minister, what is your first requirement of your Navy?"

He replied, "I want you to send as many ships as possible to Famagusta to bring over the refugees who were interned there, because we need them here in Israel". I knew that BG had a very good sense of humour and so I said to him, "May I respectfully advise against that course and suggest instead that you ask the United Nations to call for a Referendum in Famagusta as to whether they would like to join the State of Israel. After all," I said to him, "we have 300,000 there who would certainly vote to join Israel and," I continued, "if we have Haifa on the one side and Famagusta on the other, we can control this end of the Mediterranean." BG smiled at this suggestion and said, "You are a typical Britisher - we have only just got a State and you already want an Empire." Whilst I was talking to BG, Sharet[*] suddenly appeared and said he wanted to talk to BG importantly and privately and so I was asked to wait outside for a moment. It appeared that Sharet was carrying a telegram from Washington to announce that the United States had recognised the State of Israel. Thereupon, BG flung open the door and said to me, "Tikaness." When I entered the room, he told me the news and said, "You are no longer a pirate."

We proceeded immediately to set in motion the ships for carrying out BG's orders. In the meanwhile, I made fullest enquiries about Aliya Beth ships that might be on the way. I decided that we must intercept them as they approached the Israel coast because I feared that on approaching the coast, the

---

[*] Shertok, on becoming officially Foreign Minister, changed his name to Sharet.

refugees in these ships would inevitably tend to crowd the decks in order to catch sight of the Promised Land. The skies along the coast were wide open to the Egyptian Spitfires which were armed with cannon and might well be expected to attack such an Aliya Beth ship. If there was nothing to betray the exact nature of the ship, they might otherwise pass as ordinary fishing boats upon which enemy aircraft would not be inclined to waste ammunition. When I heard that one of these ships was approaching the coast, I went out with two or three of my officers to intercept. When we boarded the ship, I explained to the Kibbutz Niks who were crewing the vessel what my orders were in relation to the people they were carrying. We then went below decks and received a tremendously emotional welcome from the hundreds of people crammed in the holds who were naturally excited to see Officers of the Israeli Navy. I had deliberately taken with me an Officer who could speak Yiddish, which I could not do, so that he could explain my policy to the passengers and the reasons for it. In the result, everyone on the ships, both from Famagusta and Aliya Beth were able to reach Israel without mishap.

In setting up the necessary organisation for the Navy, one of my first tasks was to organise the obtaining and analysis of intelligence, particularly in regard to the activities of the Egyptian Navy. I chose as the Head of Intelligence section, Lova Eliav, a young man who had impressed me with his obvious ability. I knew perfectly well from my experience with the British Navy, the value and importance of intelligence. It was important to organise connections with Haganah Intelligence as in War every possible source is vital. Eventually I was satisfied that this branch of Naval work was operating efficiently, but it was always apparent that until the Navy itself could be sufficiently armed and equipped, the opportunities for taking advantage of the information we were able to accumulate were limited.

CHAPTER 12

Being used to the British way of life, it took some time for me to understand the extent and force of politics in Israeli affairs. In my philosophy and in British forces, the political views of an individual were his own affair and there had to be strong evidence of unfitness for his job in other respects to affect his career. Indeed I had experienced a case in which a petty officer who was outstandingly able but was a known communist was nevertheless given a commission and subsequent promotion. That this sort of thing was not going to happen in Israel was quickly brought home to me.

I have mentioned before that our largest ship was the armoured ex-US ice-breaker of 2500 tons which we had named ELATH. We provided for her the gun made up by dismantling one of the ex-French 65mm guns which was the only artillery that Shaul Meyeroff, our purchasing agent in Geneva, had been able to acquire. These were all desperately needed by the army and we were lucky to be spared one for our erstwhile "battleship". To command her, I had appointed a certain Captain Chodoroff who was far and away the most qualified sailor we had found. He had British and Italian training and a full Masters ticket. Having sent him to sea, I was greatly surprised and shocked to be told after a day or two that on the direct orders of Ben Gurion the ship and been recalled and Chodoroff removed as being politically unreliable. When I protested to BG, he patiently explained to me the serious situation that had arisen over the stubborn refusal of the Irgun to submit to the discipline of the regular army and merge fully and loyally with the forces of the State. This problem had arisen during the attack on Jaffa and was becoming more acute and indeed was to lead to the terrible events of the "Altalena".

If we were to face virtual mutiny of this kind, I clearly had to accept the Prime Minister's ruling and moreover I saw the wisdom of having my Histatadruth "guru".

It was the Altalena incident which finally taught the lesson of disunity. The Irgun party had chartered the Altalena to carry to Israel a large quantity of armaments which they had been able to acquire in Europe. The Captain of the ship was Captain Halpern who had been the head of our ORT training ship at Erith on Thames and was consequently well known to me. As his ship approached the Israeli coast, he was ordered by the Government to surrender the Altalena and her cargo to the regular army. This the Irgun refused to do. Reluctantly the order had to be issued to the army to seize the ship by force and if there was armed resistance from the Irgun, there was to be no hesitation in opening fire. In consequence a pitched battle ensued in which Jew had to fire on Jew. The outcome was of course that the army triumphed and an end of the Irgun mutiny was achieved.

What tasks could our little navy usefully perform in the gigantic struggle for survival in which we were now engulfed? Aggression was clearly out of the question. Indeed I had sent a small craft to gather information about the Egyptian landings in the area of Gaza. Fortunately, our scout was not attacked by the destroyers escorting the troops which were being landed on the beaches of Gaza. These destroyers were of the Tribal class and were ex Royal Navy ships sold to Egypt. How I longed to have something to attack them, but we had nothing. We had plans to make rocket launchers but there had been no time or resources to make them.

Apart from intelligence gathering, there were the escort plans for immigrant ships and these were all successfully accomplished.

Our part in the taking of Jaffa, I have already described. The other function I had envisaged was to provide mobility for the army. This became a vital task in the taking of the Galil.

The situation in Galilee was that there were a number of smaller army units fighting in various parts. The Lebanese army had advanced for a short distance. The Syrian army was also attacking. A small irregular force under Fawzi el Kaukji was blocked as Dayan has vividly described in his biography. Other Arab forces were besieging Naharea and Acre was entirely in Arab hands.

In these circumstances, Mickey Marcus the American volunteer was advising the army. He called for more concentration of forces and a planned attacking campaign. Here as I saw it was the opportunity for the navy to carry out its role. We therefore undertook to land troops at night behind these various Arab groups. At Ras en Nakoura on the Lebanese frontier, there was a railway bridge. There at night we landed a force which blew up the bridge and was in position behind the Lebanese army. Further down the coast, other of our ships landed troops behind the Arabs around Naharea. Other landings were outside Acre to link up with the force advancing from Haifa around the Bay of Acre. Daylight therefore found the situation markedly changed. The Lebanese, finding themselves cut off, retreated hurriedly, leaving us in possession of a vast quantity of valuable material.

The Arabs lifted the siege of Naharea. Acre was closely invested but fierce fighting ensued before the strong central citadel was at last taken. The Syrians had retreated after their attack on Dagania had cost them the loss of a tank. Likewise Fawzi el Kaukji had withdrawn his irregulars after suffering considerably from army attacks. At last the Galil was ours.

I was pleased to think that my navy had proved the value of mobility. If only we could have added a naval bombardment to the night's work as I had seen at the Seine Bay assault.

CHAPTER 13

By June 1948 it had become apparent to the Arabs that Israel was not going to be destroyed as easily as they had imagined. Moves were afoot to bring about a truce. It was not until the end of June that a truce was finally arranged. In the meantime I had serious discussions with Ben Gurion about my own position. I had been officially appointed "Naval Adviser to the State of Israel". I had been offered the highest Naval rank, but this involved the relinquishing of my British nationality and the adoption of Israeli citizenship. One could not possibly hold a commission in the Israeli forces otherwise. BG urged me to make the decision and stay on as a regular officer or at least to remain in Israel as the official advisor. I pointed out to him that I could only consider remaining in that capacity if some remuneration could be provided. Until that moment, all my services had been freely given and like many other volunteers we were happy to accept the opportunity to serve without material reward. The spiritual satisfaction of helping to establish the State was enough, but could only be so on a short term basis. Ben Gurion was very understanding and expressed gratitude for what I had achieved and sorrow at my decision to return home. We parted on the most cordial terms and as I left he said, "Bring your wife and children here to us." But he still had no suggestion of pay.

Making arrangements to leave was not simple. There were still no airlines serving the country. Ultimately I was able to cadge a lift in one of the JU52 planes that were bringing supplies of arms from Czechoslovakia and returning empty. Fuel being in short supply, we were only permitted to load enough to get us to Cyprus where we filled our tanks. Next stop was Rome from where I could get a normal flight to London.

After my return to London, I learned that BG had in fact received an offer from an influential American quarter of the services of a young American Jewish officer who had just graduated from Annapolis, the American Naval academy, who was willing to take on in a voluntary capacity my work as Naval advisor. For my own part, I was glad to know that some professional advice would be available to the Navy I had established. I had made up my mind that I would not be happy under the circumstances that then prevailed in Israel. For one thing the evident "protectsia" on party lines governed every aspect of the establishment there was anathema to me. For example, the Minister dealing with shipping was a Mr Meyerowitz who was a brother-in-law of Sharet, but apart from being a good party man had no qualifications for the job. He certainly knew nothing about shipping or maritime matters.

Furthermore the influence of the Histatadruth and of socialist ideals was overwhelming. An illustration of this became apparent in my effort later to get Haifa developed as a primary Mediterranean port. There was at that time an urgent requirement for ship repair facilities to be available in the Eastern Mediterranean. This can be a valuable economic asset. To attract this trade Haifa would need a dry-dock. I learned from the British Admiralty that they had available a floating dock at Massawa in North Africa which they were anxious to get rid of and which they were willing to sell to Israel at a scrap price to include towing it to Haifa. This offer was rejected on the ground that a bigger dock was required. I then got an offer from the British company that had recently completed the large dry-dock at the Gibraltar dockyard to construct a similar dock in Haifa free of charge, if they could be allocated a site by the Haifa municipality with a long lease at a nominal rent to make their investment viable. I returned to Israel in December 1948 to urge on the Israel government the desirability of accepting this unique offer, but was met with the response that Israel was not going to permit capitalist exploitation!! So the opportunity was lost and was promptly taken up by Genoa which rapidly built up a thriving ship building and repairing trade. This narrow Middle European socialist ideology was typical of an attitude even of Ben Gurion himself, though in other respects he was of undoubted greatness.

CHAPTER 14

EPILOGUE

The State of Israel today is substantially a very different country from the one I have described in 1948. For one thing of course, the initial pioneering fervour which emphasised so many East European ideas and largely accepted the dogmas of socialism has mainly disappeared and, freed from those shackles, a healthy and prosperous economy has been developed.

Looking back to the War of Liberation and the events of 1948, the one cause of personal satisfaction to me is the simple fact that the Israeli Navy has developed and is now a valued part of the armed forces of the State. It was gratifying to read in the autobiography of Moshe Dayan in describing the events of the Yom Kippur war the following: -

> "The Israeli Navy was very active in this war. In general, no emphasis was given to our naval forces in any of Israel's earlier campaigns. Our borders with all our neighbours are land borders and as a rule there has been no pressing need to attack Syria or Egypt from the sea - the Mediterranean and the Gulf of Suez - or to take any extraordinary defensive measures against possible seaborne attacks by the enemy. But thanks to the fighting spirit and initiative of the Commander of the Navy and his men, our small fleet of fast missile boats carried out a number of dashing operations. They simply thrust themselves into Egyptian and Syrian naval bases seeking - and finding - opportunities to enter into battle with the enemy vessels which were armed with Soviet missiles.

To overcome the advantage of range of these Soviet missiles, our boats had to approach their targets at speed - to hit them before the enemy could activate his missiles - or shoot down the enemy missile while it was still in the air. The Navy was splendid."

All this was high praise from a soldier, though I think it obviously omits the valuable services of the Navy on many previous occasions. But having like Cincinnatus "returned to the plough", I can now only watch and observe from afar.